FIRST 50 CHRISTMAS CAROLS
YOU SHOULD PLAY ON UKULELE

Angels from the Realms of Glory 2

Angels We Have Heard on High 4

As with Gladness Men of Old 3

Auld Lang Syne 6

Away in a Manger 7

Bring a Torch, Jeannette, Isabella 8

A Child Is Born in Bethlehem 10

Christ Was Born on Christmas Day 11

Come, Thou Long-Expected Jesus 12

Coventry Carol 14

Deck the Hall 16

Ding Dong! Merrily on High! 15

The First Noël 18

The Friendly Beasts 20

Fum, Fum, Fum 22

Go, Tell It on the Mountain 23

God Rest Ye Merry, Gentlemen 24

Good Christian Men, Rejoice 26

Good King Wenceslas 28

Hark! The Herald Angels Sing 30

He Is Born, the Holy Child 32

Here We Come A-Wassailing 34

The Holly and the Ivy 36

I Heard the Bells on Christmas Day 37

I Saw Three Ships 38

In the Bleak M[...] 39

Infant Holy, Inf[...] 40

It Came Upon the Midnight Clear 42

Jingle Bells 44

Jolly Old St. Nicholas 41

Joy to the World 46

O Christmas Tree 47

O Come, All Ye Faithful 48

O Come, Little Children 49

O Come, O Come, Emmanuel 50

O Holy Night 52

O Little Town of Bethlehem 51

Once in Royal David's City 54

Pat-a-Pan 55

Silent Night 56

Star of the East 58

Still, Still, Still 57

Sussex Carol 60

The Twelve Days of Christmas 62

Ukrainian Bell Carol 64

Up on the Housetop 66

We Three Kings of Orient Are 68

We Wish You a Merry Christmas 67

What Child Is This? 70

While Shepherds Watched Their Flocks 72

ISBN 978-1-4950-9607-5

7777 W. BLUEMOUND RD. P.O. BOX 13819 MILWAUKEE, WI 53213

In Australia Contact:
Hal Leonard Australia Pty. Ltd.
4 Lentara Court
Cheltenham, Victoria, 3192 Australia
Email: ausadmin@halleonard.com.au

Visit Hal Leonard Online at
www.halleonard.com

Angels from the Realms of Glory

Words by James Montgomery
Music by Henry T. Smart

As with Gladness Men of Old

Words by William Chatterton Dix
Music by Conrad Kocher

Angels We Have Heard on High

Traditional French Carol
Translated by James Chadwick

First note

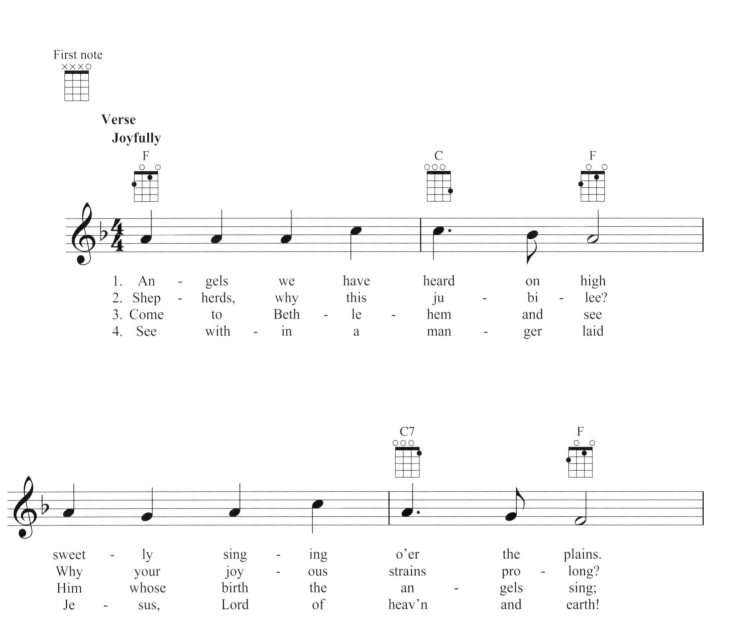

1. An - gels we have heard on high
2. Shep - herds, why this ju - bi - lee?
3. Come to Beth - le - hem and see
4. See with - in a man - ger laid

sweet - ly sing - ing o'er the plains.
Why your joy - ous strains pro - long?
Him whose birth the an - gels sing;
Je - sus, Lord of heav'n and earth!

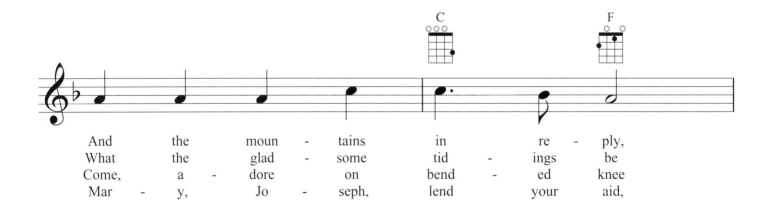

And the moun - tains in re - ply,
What the glad - some tid - ings be
Come, a - dore on bend - ed knee
Mar - y, Jo - seph, lend your aid,

ech - o - ing their joy - ous strains.
which in - spire your heav - 'nly song?
Christ the Lord, the new - born King.
with us sing our Sav - ior's birth.

Chorus

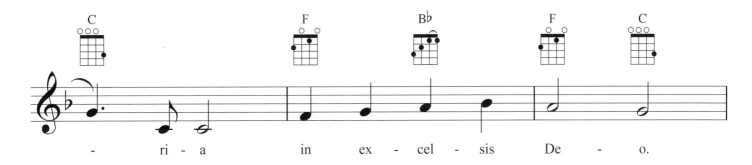

Glo - -

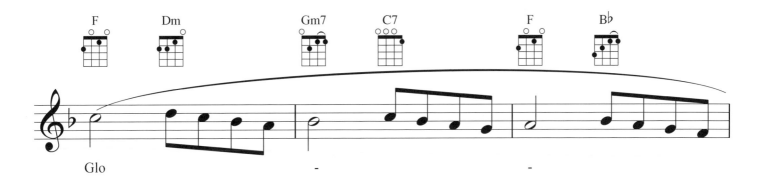

- ri - a in ex - cel - sis De - o.

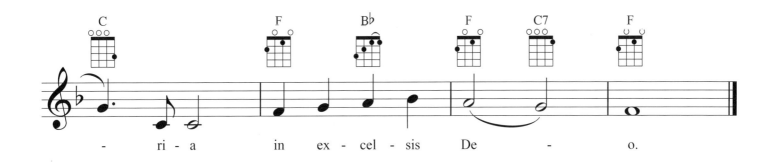

Glo - -

- ri - a in ex - cel - sis De - o.

Auld Lang Syne

Words by Robert Burns
Traditional Scottish Melody

Away in a Manger

Words by John T. McFarland (v. 3)
Music by James R. Murray

First note

Verse
Sweetly

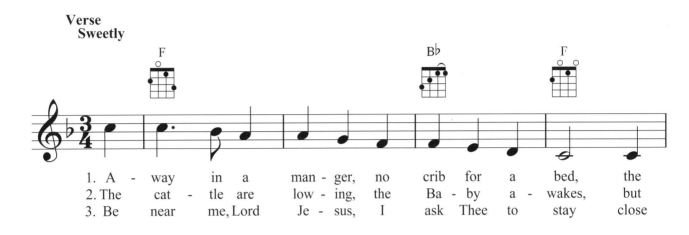

1. A - way in a man - ger, no crib for a bed, the
2. The cat - tle are low - ing, the Ba - by a - wakes, but
3. Be near me, Lord Je - sus, I ask Thee to stay close

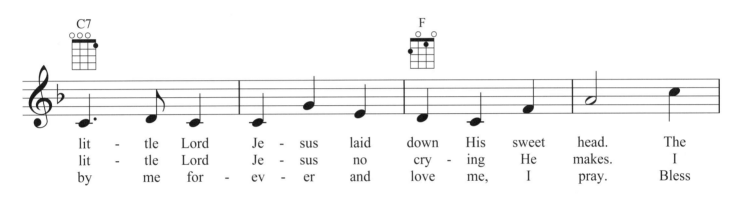

lit - tle Lord Je - sus laid down His sweet head. The
lit - tle Lord Je - sus no cry - ing He makes. I
by me for - ev - er and love me, I pray. Bless

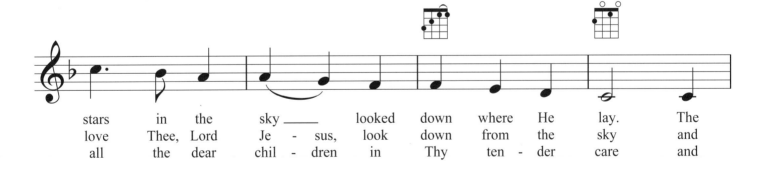

stars in the sky _____ looked down where He lay. The
love Thee, Lord Je - sus, look down from the sky The and
all the dear chil - dren in Thy ten - der care and

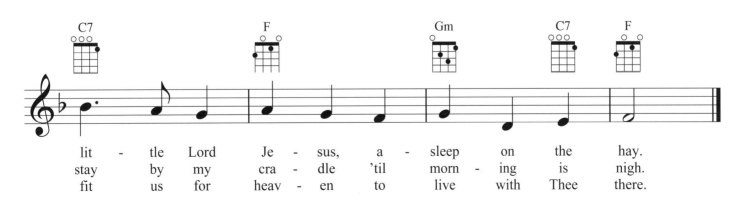

lit - tle Lord Je - sus, a - sleep on the hay.
stay by my cra - dle 'til morn - ing is nigh.
fit us for heav - en to live with Thee there.

Bring a Torch, Jeannette, Isabella

17th Century French Provençal Carol

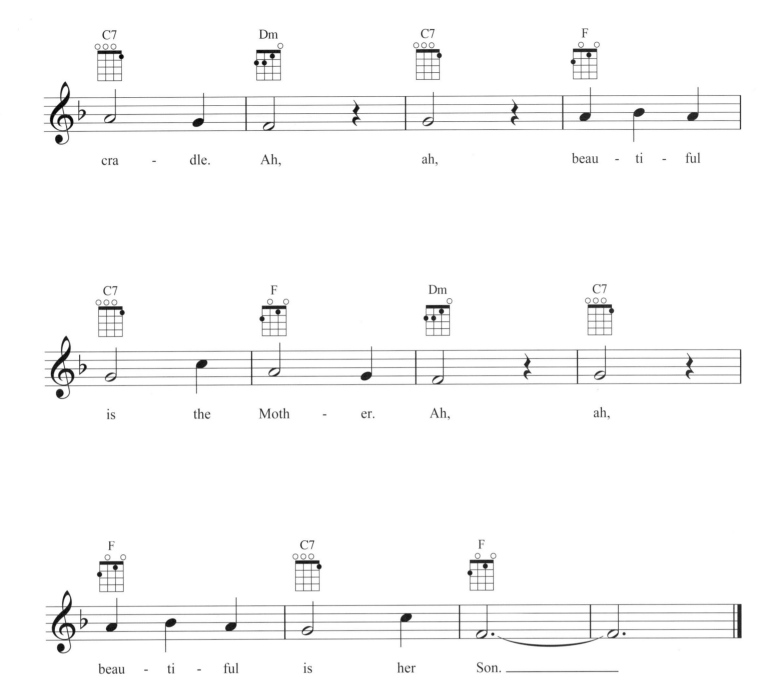

cra - dle. Ah, ah, beau - ti - ful

is the Moth - er. Ah, ah,

beau - ti - ful is her Son. _____

Additional Lyrics

2. Hasten now, good folk of the village,
   Hasten now, the Christ Child to see.
   You will find Him asleep in a manger,
   Quietly come and whisper softly.
   Hush, hush, peacefully now He slumbers,
   Hush, hush, peacefully now He sleeps.

A Child Is Born in Bethlehem

14th-Century Latin Text adapted by Nicolai F.S. Grundtvig
Traditional Danish Melody

First note

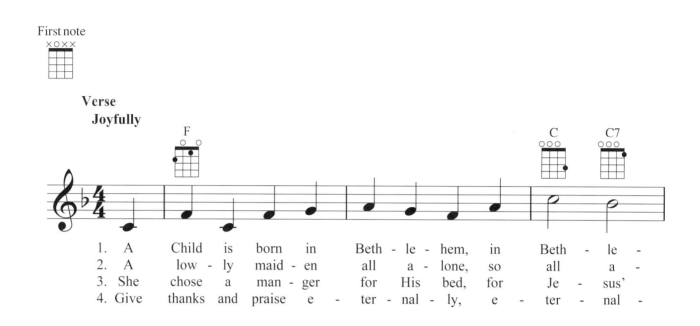

Verse
Joyfully

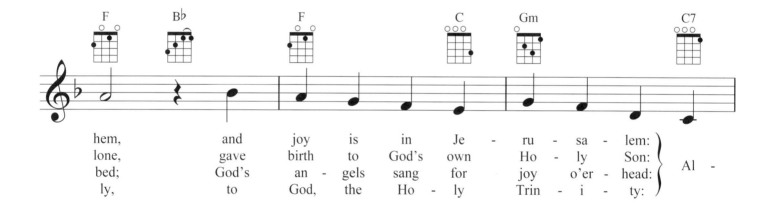

1. A   Child is   born in   Beth - le - hem, in   Beth - le -
2. A   low - ly maid - en   all a - lone, so   all a -
3. She chose a   man - ger for His bed, for Je - sus'
4. Give thanks and praise e - ter - nal - ly, e - ter - nal -

hem,   and   joy   is   in   Je - ru - sa - lem:
lone,   gave   birth to   God's   own   Ho - ly Son:
bed;   God's an - gels sang   for   joy o'er - head: } Al -
ly,   to   God,   the   Ho - ly   Trin - i - ty:

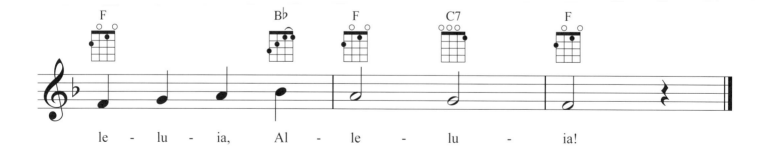

le - lu - ia, Al - le - lu - ia!

Christ Was Born on Christmas Day

Traditional

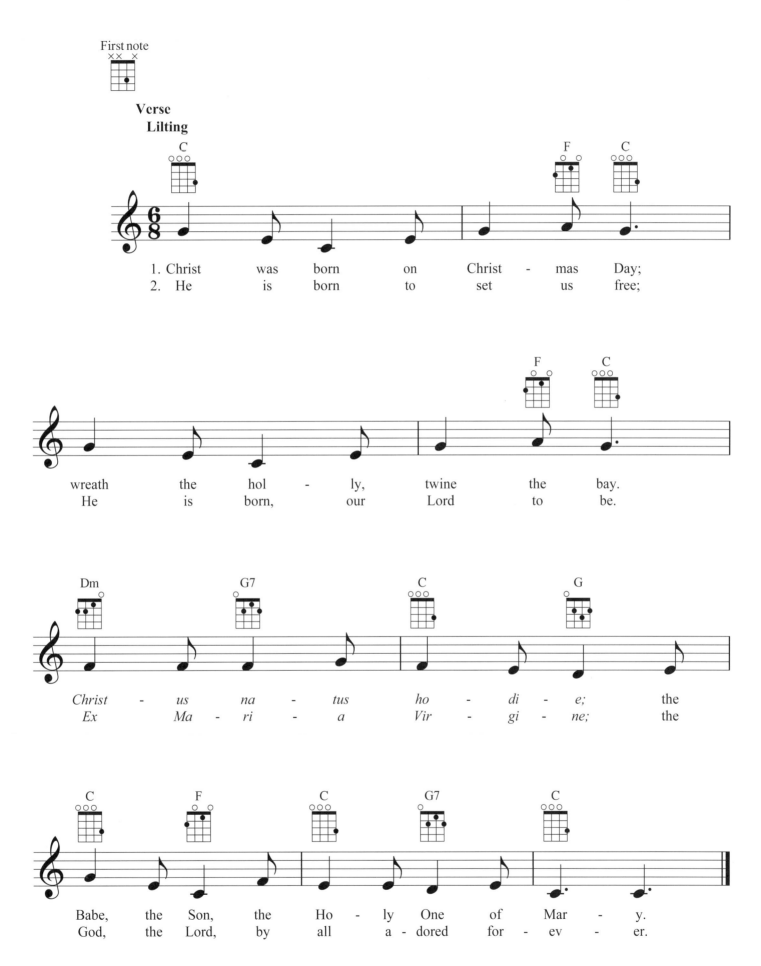

Come, Thou Long-Expected Jesus

Words by Charles Wesley
Music by Rowland Hugh Prichard

First note

Verse
Moderately fast

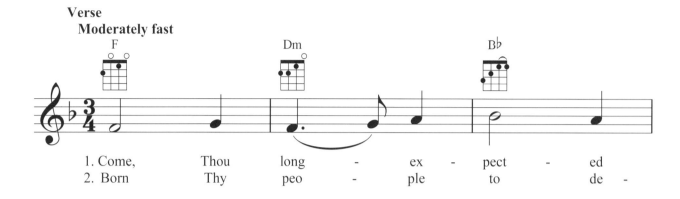

1. Come,   Thou   long -   ex - pect - ed
2. Born   Thy   peo -   ple   to   de -

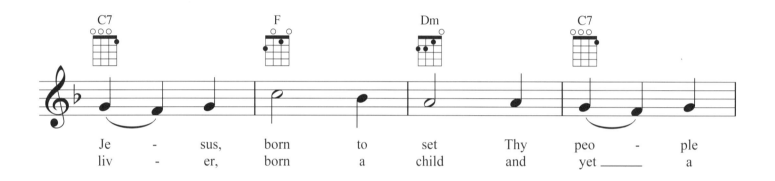

Je -   sus,   born   to   set   Thy   peo -   ple
liv -   er,   born   a   child   and   yet _____ a

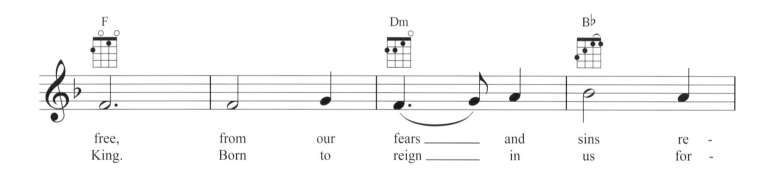

free,   from   our   fears _____ and   sins   re -
King.   Born   to   reign _____ in   us   for -

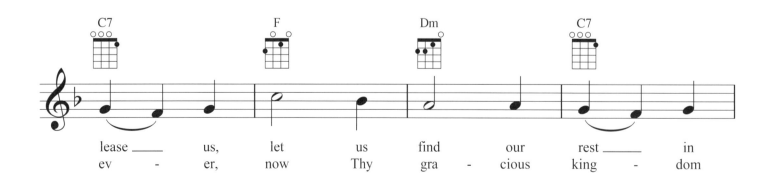

lease _____ us,   let   us   find   our   rest _____ in
ev -   er,   now   Thy   gra - cious   king - dom

Coventry Carol

Words by Robert Croo
Traditional English Melody

Additional Lyrics

3. Herod the king, in his raging,
   Charged he hath this day
   His men of might, in his own sight,
   All young children to slay.

4. That woe is me, poor Child, for Thee!
   And ever morn and day,
   For Thy parting neither say nor sing,
   By, by, lully, lullay.

Ding Dong! Merrily on High!

Traditional French Carol

1. Ding dong! Mer - ri - ly on high in heav'n the bells are
2., 3. *See additional lyrics*

ring - ing. Ding dong! Ver - i - ly the sky is riv'n with an - gel

sing - ing. Glo -

- - -

- ri - a! Ho - san - na in ex - cel - sis!

Additional Lyrics

2. E'en so here below, below, let steeple bells be swinging.
   And i-o, i-o, i-o, by priest and people singing.

3. Pray you, dutifully prime your matin chime, ye ringers.
   May you beautiful rime your evetime song, ye singers.

Deck the Hall

Traditional Welsh Carol

First note

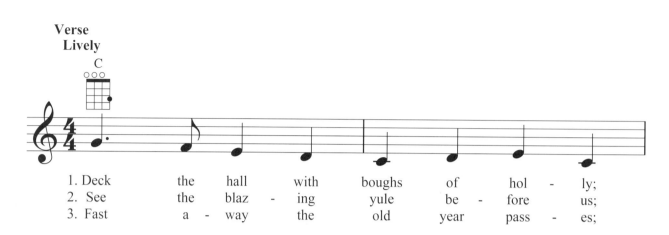

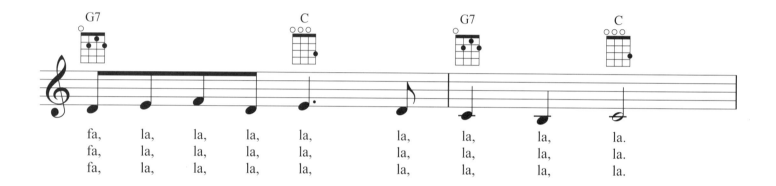

1. Deck the hall with boughs of hol - ly;
2. See the blaz - ing yule be - fore us;
3. Fast a - way the old year pass - es;

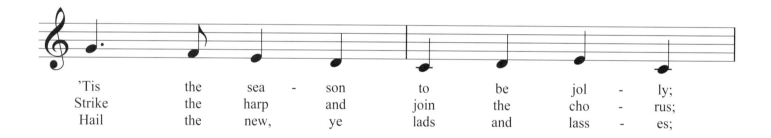

fa, la, la, la, la, la, la, la, la.
fa, la, la, la, la, la, la, la, la.
fa, la, la, la, la, la, la, la, la.

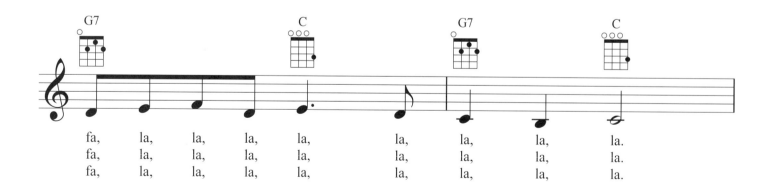

'Tis the sea - son to be jol - ly;
Strike the harp and join the cho - rus;
Hail the new, ye lads and lass - es;

fa, la, la, la, la, la, la, la, la.
fa, la, la, la, la, la, la, la, la.
fa, la, la, la, la, la, la, la, la.

G7						C		
Don	we	now	our	gay	ap	-	par	-	el;
Fol	-	low	me	in	mer	-	ry	meas	-	ure;
Sing	we	joy	-	ous	all	to	-	geth	-	er;

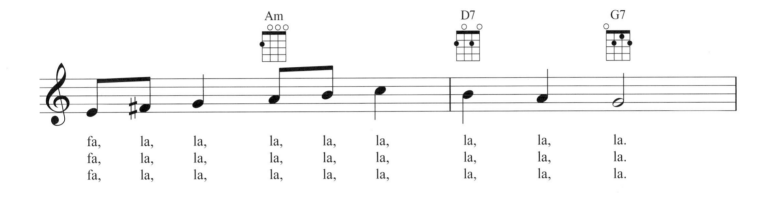

			Am			D7		G7
fa,	la,	la,	la,	la,	la,	la,	la,	la.
fa,	la,	la,	la,	la,	la,	la,	la,	la.
fa,	la,	la,	la,	la,	la,	la,	la,	la.

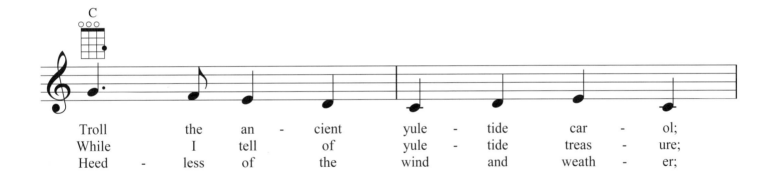

C								
Troll	the	an	-	cient	yule	-	tide	car	-	ol;
While	I	tell	of	yule	-	tide	treas	-	ure;
Heed	-	less	of	the	wind	and	weath	-	er;

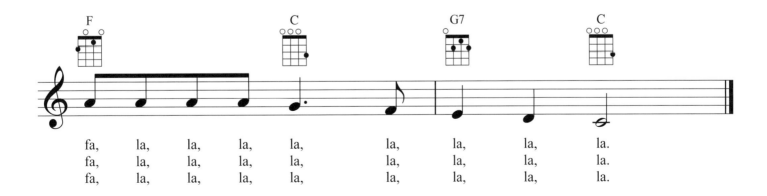

F					C		G7	C
fa,	la,	la,	la,	la,	la,	la,	la,	la.
fa,	la,	la,	la,	la,	la,	la,	la,	la.
fa,	la,	la,	la,	la,	la,	la,	la,	la.

The First Noël

17th Century English Carol
Music from W. Sandys' *Christmas Carols*

First note

Moderately

Verse

1. The ___ first _____ No - ël the ___ an - gel did
(2.–5.) *See additional lyrics*

say, was to cer - tain poor shep - herds in

fields as they lay; in _____ fields _____ where ___

they lay ___ keep - ing their sheep, on a

cold win - ter's night ___ that was ___ so deep. No -

Chorus

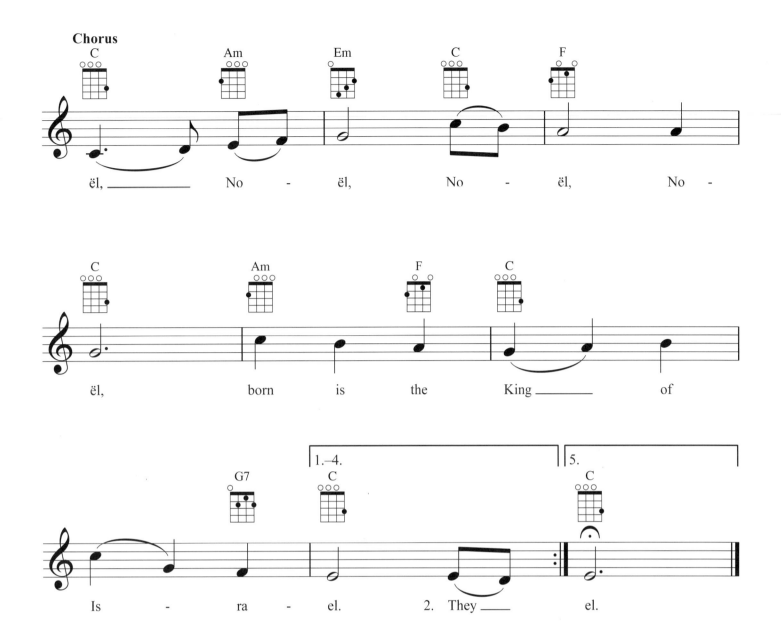

ël, _____ No - ël, No - ël, No - ël, born is the King _____ of Is - ra - el. 2. They _____ el.

Additional Lyrics

2. They looked up and saw a star
   Shining in the east, beyond them far;
   And to the earth it gave great light
   And so it continued both day and night.

3. And by the light of that same star,
   Three wise men came from country far;
   To seek for a King was their intent,
   And to follow the star wherever it went.

4. This star drew nigh to the northwest,
   O'er Bethlehem it took its rest;
   And there it did both stop and stay,
   Right over the place where Jesus lay.

5. Then entered in those wise men three,
   Full reverently upon their knee;
   And offered there in His presence,
   Their gold and myrrh and frankincense.

The Friendly Beasts

Traditional English Carol

First note

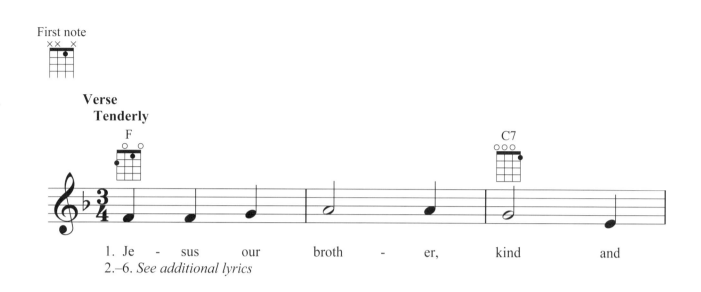

1. Je - sus our broth - er, kind and
2.–6. *See additional lyrics*

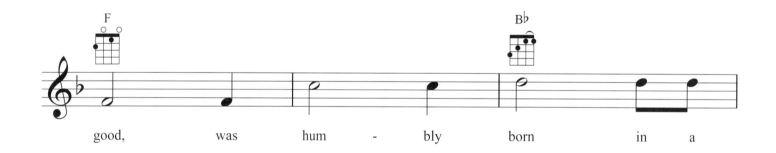

good, was hum - bly born in a

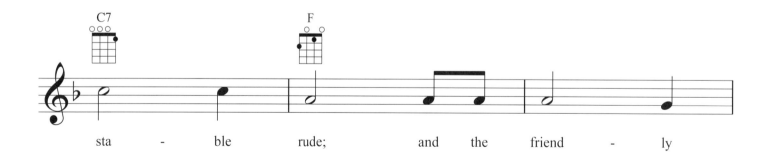

sta - ble rude; and the friend - ly

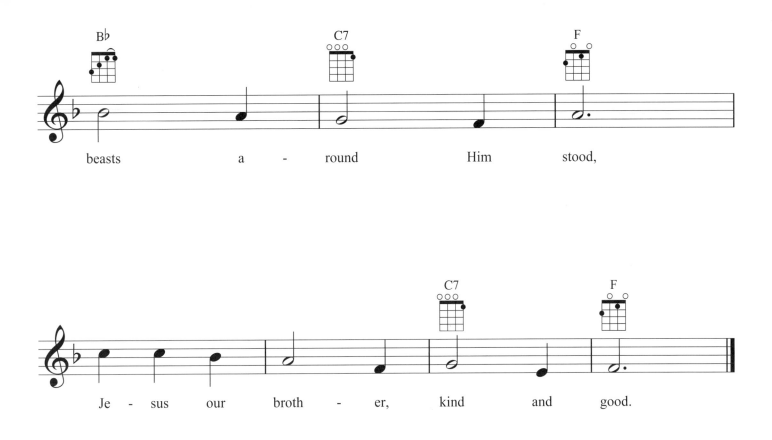

beasts a - round Him stood,

Je - sus our broth - er, kind and good.

Additional Lyrics

2. "I," said the donkey, shaggy and brown,
   "I carried His mother up hill and down.
   I carried His mother to Bethlehem town."
   "I," said the donkey, shaggy and brown.

3. "I," said the cow, all white and red,
   "I gave Him my manger for His bed.
   I gave Him my hay to pillow His head."
   "I," said the cow, all white and red.

4. "I," said the sheep with the curly horn,
   "I gave Him my wool for His blanket warm.
   He wore my coat on Christmas morn."
   "I," said the sheep with the curly horn.

5. "I," said the dove from the rafters high,
   "I cooed Him to sleep that He would not cry.
   We cooed Him to sleep, my mate and I."
   "I," said the dove from the rafters high.

6. Thus every beast by some good spell,
   In the stable dark was glad to tell
   Of the gift he gave Emmanuel,
   The gift he gave Emmanuel.

Fum, Fum, Fum

Traditional Catalonian Carol

Go, Tell It on the Mountain

African-American Spiritual
Verses by John W. Work, Jr.

Chorus
Brightly

Go, tell it on the moun - tain, o - ver the hills and

ev - 'ry - where. Go, tell it on the moun - tain that

Last time Fine

Je - sus Christ __ is born.

Verse

1. While shep - herds kept their
2. The shep - herds feared and
3. Down in a low - ly

watch - ing o'er si - lent flocks by night, be - hold! through - out the
trem - bled when, lo! a - bove the earth rang out the an - gel
man - ger the hum - ble Christ was born, and God sent us sal -

D.C.

heav - ens there shone a ho - ly light. _____
cho - rus that hailed our Sav - ior's birth. _____
va - tion that bless - ed Christ - mas morn. _____

God Rest Ye Merry, Gentlemen

19th Century English Carol

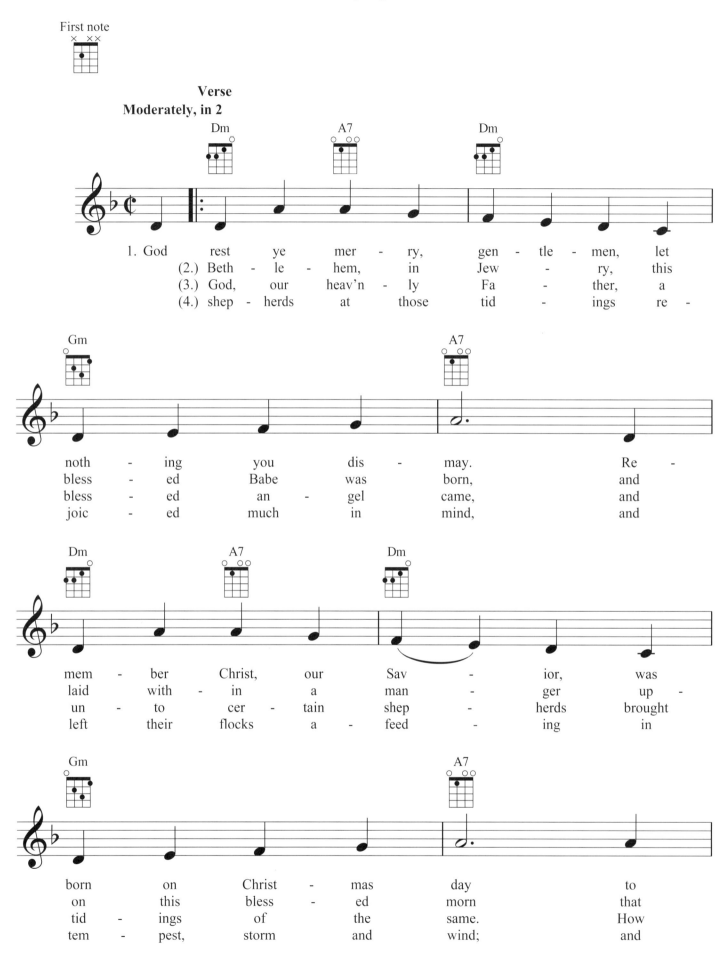

save us all from Sa - tan's pow'r when
which His moth - er Mar - y did
that in Beth - le - hem was born the
went to Beth - le - hem straight - way the

we were gone a - stray.
noth - ing take in scorn.
Son of God by name.
Son of God to find.

O _____

Chorus

tid - ings of com - fort and joy, com - fort and

joy. O _____ tid - ings of com - fort and

| 1.–3. | 4. |

joy. _____
2. In _____
3. From
4. Now

Good Christian Men, Rejoice

14th Century Latin Text
Translated by John Mason Neale
14th Century German Melody

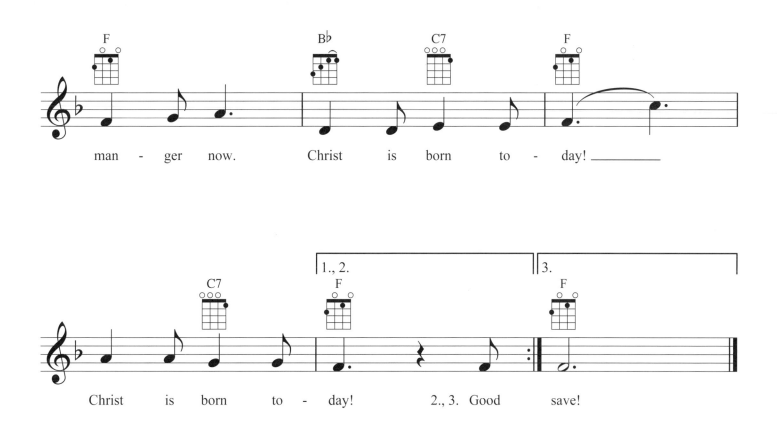

man - ger now. Christ is born to - day! _____

Christ is born to - day! 2., 3. Good save!

Additional Lyrics

2. Good Christian men, rejoice
   With heart and soul and voice.
   Now ye hear of endless bliss: Joy! Joy!
   Jesus Christ was born for this.
   He hath op'd the heavenly door,
   And man is blessed evermore.
   Christ was born for this!
   Christ was born for this!

3. Good Christian men, rejoice
   With heart and soul and voice.
   Now ye need not fear the grave: Peace! Peace!
   Jesus Christ was born to save!
   Calls you one and calls you all,
   To gain His everlasting hall.
   Christ was born to save!
   Christ was born to save!

Good King Wenceslas

Words by John M. Neale
Music from *Piae Cantiones*

C   F   Dm   B♭   C7

Bright - ly shone the moon that night, though the frost was
"Sire, he lives a good league hence, un - der - neath the
Page and mon - arch forth they went, forth they went to -

F   B♭   Dm   C

cru - el; when a poor man came in sight,
moun - tain; right a - gainst the for - est fence,
geth - er; through the rude wind's wild la - ment

F   C   Dm   B♭   F

gath - 'ring win - ter fu - el.
by St. Ag - nes foun - tain."
and the bit - ter weath - er.

Additional Lyrics

4. "Sire, the night is darker now,
   And the wind blows stronger;
   Fails my heart, I know not how,
   I can go no longer."
   "Mark my footsteps, my good page,
   Tread thou in them boldly;
   Thou shalt find the winter's rage
   Freeze thy blood less coldly."

5. In his master's steps he trod,
   Where the snow lay dinted;
   Heat was in the very sod
   Which the saint has printed.
   Therefore, Christmas men, be sure,
   Wealth or rank possessing;
   Ye who now will bless the poor
   Shall yourselves find blessing.

Hark! The Herald Angels Sing

Words by Charles Wesley
Altered by George Whitefield
Music by Felix Mendelssohn-Bartholdy
Arranged by William H. Cummings

F				B♭		C	

join the tri - umph of the skies. _____
hail th'in - car - nate De - i - ty. _____
born that man no more may die. _____

B♭				D		Gm	

With th'an - gel - ic hosts pro - claim,
Pleased as man with man to dwell,
Born to raise with the sons of earth,

C7		F				C7	F

"Christ is _____ born in Beth - le - hem." }
Je - sus, _____ our Im - man - u - el. }
born to _____ give them sec - ond birth. }

Chorus

B♭				D		Gm	

Hark! the her - ald an - gels sing,

C7		F		1., 2. C7	F	3. C7	F

"Glo - ry _____ to the new - born King!" new - born King!"

He Is Born, the Holy Child

(Il est ne, le divin enfant)

Traditional French Carol

Verse

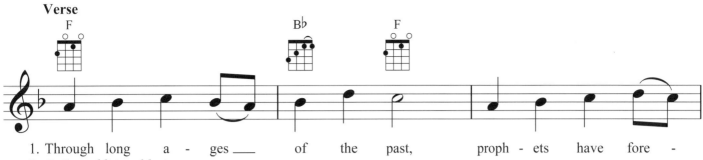

1. Through long a - ges ___ of the past, proph - ets have fore -
2., 3. *See additional lyrics*

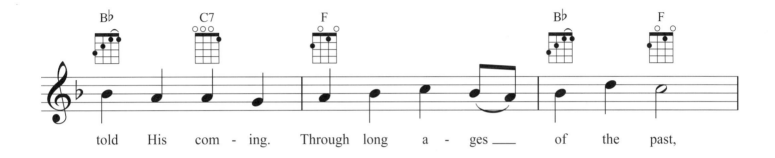

told His com - ing. Through long a - ges ___ of the past,

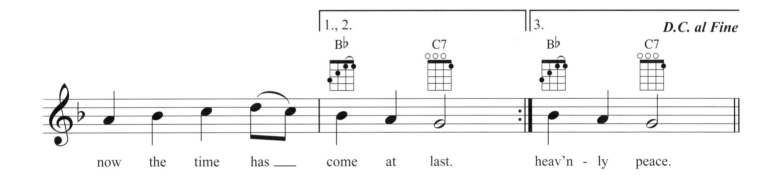

1., 2.   3.   ***D.C. al Fine***

now the time has ___ come at last.   heav'n - ly peace.

Additional Lyrics

2. Oh, how lovely, oh, how pure
   Is this perfect Child of heaven.
   Oh, how lovely, oh, how pure,
   Gracious gift of God to man.

3. Jesus, Lord of all the world,
   Coming as a child among us.
   Jesus, Lord of all the world,
   Grant to us Thy heav'nly peace.

Here We Come A-Wassailing

Traditional

First note

Verse
Brightly

1. Here we come a - was - sail - ing a -
(2.) are not dai - ly beg - gars that
3. We have got a lit - tle purse of
(4.) bless the mas - ter of this house, like -

mong the leaves so green.
beg from door to door, but
stretch - ing leath - er skin; we
wise the mis - tress, too; and

Here we come a - wan - d'ring, so fair _____ to be
we are neigh - bor chil - dren whom you have seen be -
want a lit - tle mon - ey to line the well with -
all the lit - tle chil - dren that round the ta - ble

The Holly and the Ivy

18th Century English Carol

Additional Lyrics

2. The holly bears a blossom
   As white as lily flow'r,
   And Mary bore sweet Jesus Christ,
   To be our sweet Savior.

3. The holly bears a berry
   As red as any blood,
   And Mary bore sweet Jesus Christ,
   To do poor sinners good.

I Heard the Bells on Christmas Day

Words by Henry Wadsworth Longfellow
Music by John Baptiste Calkin

First note

Verse

Moderately

1. I heard the bells on Christ - mas day, their old fa - mil - iar
(2.) thought how as the day had come, the bel - fries of all
(3.–5.) *See additional lyrics*

car - ols play; and mild and sweet the words re - peat, of
Chris - ten - dom had rolled a - long th'un - bro - ken song of

peace on earth, good will to men. 2. I will to men.
peace on earth, good will to men. 3. And

Additional Lyrics

3. And in despair I bowed my head:
   "There is no peace on earth," I said,
   "For hate is strong, and mocks the song
   Of peace on earth, good will to men."

4. Then pealed the bells more loud and deep:
   "God is not dead, nor doth He sleep;
   The wrong shall fail, the right prevail,
   With peace on earth, good will to men."

5. Till ringing, singing on its way,
   The world revolved from night to day,
   A voice, a chime, a chant sublime,
   Of peace on earth, good will to men!

I Saw Three Ships

Traditional English Carol

First note

Verse

Spirited

1. I saw three ships come sail - ing in on Christ - mas Day, on
(2.) what was in those ships all three on Christ - mas Day, on

Christ - mas Day. I saw three ships come sail - ing in on
Christ - mas Day? And saw what was in those ships all three on

Verse

Christ - mas Day in the morn - ing. 2. And
Christ - mas Day in the morn - ing? 3. The Vir - gin Mar - y and

Christ were there on Christ - mas Day, on Christ - mas Day. The

Vir - gin Mar - y and Christ were there on Christ - mas Day in the morn - ing.

In the Bleak Midwinter

Poem by Christina Rossetti
Music by Gustav Holst

Infant Holy, Infant Lowly

Traditional Polish Carol
Paraphrased by Edith M.G. Reed

Jolly Old St. Nicholas

Traditional 19th Century American Carol

Additional Lyrics

2. When the clock is striking twelve, when I'm fast asleep,
   Down the chimney broad and black, with your pack you'll creep.
   All the stockings you will find hanging in a row.
   Mine will be the shortest one, you'll be sure to know.

3. Johnny wants a pair of skates; Susy wants a sled.
   Nellie wants a picture book, yellow, blue and red.
   Now I think I'll leave to you what to give the rest.
   Choose for me, dear Santa Claus. You will know the best.

It Came Upon the Midnight Clear

Words by Edmund Hamilton Sears
Music by Richard Storrs Willis

First note

Verse
Flowing

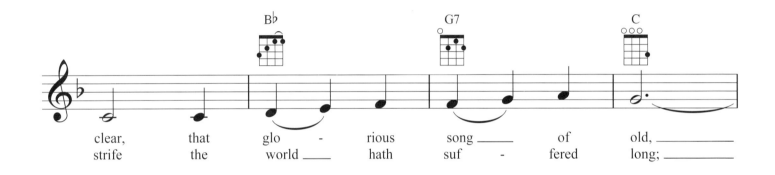

1. It came up - on _____ the mid - night
2. Yet with the woes _____ of sin and
3., 4. *See additional lyrics*

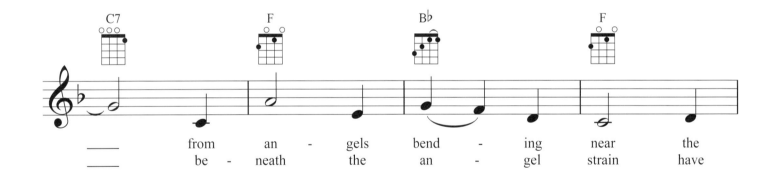

clear, that glo - rious song _____ of old, _____
strife that the world _____ hath suf - fered long; _____

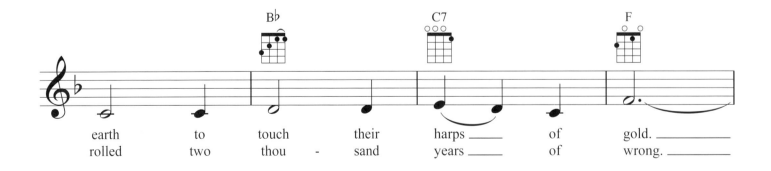

_____ from an - gels bend - ing near the
_____ be - neath the an - gel strain have

earth to touch their harps _____ of gold. _____
rolled two thou - sand years _____ of wrong. _____

Additional Lyrics

3. And ye, beneath life's crushing load,
   Whose forms are bending low,
   Who toil along the climbing way
   With painful steps and slow;
   Look now, for glad and golden hours
   Come swiftly on the wing.
   O rest beside the weary road
   And hear the angels sing.

4. For lo, the days are hast'ning on,
   By prophet bards foretold,
   When with the ever-circling years
   Comes round the age of gold;
   When peace shall over all the earth
   Its ancient splendors fling,
   And the whole world give back the song
   Which now the angels sing.

Jingle Bells

Words and Music by J. Pierpont

Chorus

Joy to the World

Words by Isaac Watts
Music by George Frideric Handel
Adapted by Lowell Mason

Verse
Brightly

1. Joy to the world! The Lord is come; let earth re-
2. Joy to the world! The Sav - ior reigns; let men their
3. No more let sin and sor - row grow; nor thorns in - the
4. He rules the world with truth and grace, and makes the

ceive her King; let ev - 'ry heart pre - pare Him
songs em - ploy; while fields and floods, rocks, hills and
fest the ground; He comes to make His bless - ings
na - tions prove the glo - ries of His right - eous -

room, and heav'n and na - ture sing, and heav'n and na - ture
plains re - peat the sound - ing joy, re - peat the sound - ing
flow, far as the curse is found, far as the curse is
ness, and won - ders of His love, and won - ders of His

sing, and heav'n and heav'n and na - ture sing.
joy, re - peat, re - peat the sound - ing joy.
found, far as, far as the curse is found.
love, and won - ders, and won - ders of His love.

O Christmas Tree

Traditional German Carol

O Come, All Ye Faithful

Music by John Francis Wade
Latin Words translated by Frederick Oakeley

O Come, Little Children

Words by C. von Schmidt
Music by J.P.A. Schulz

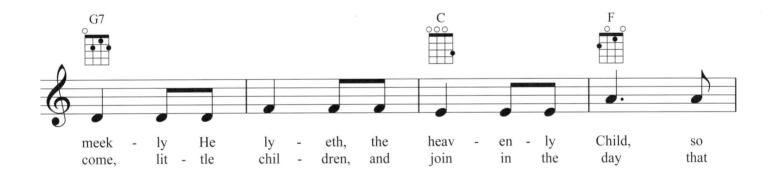

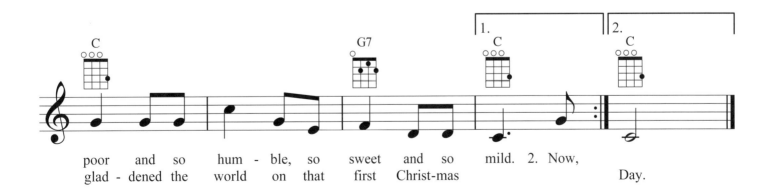

O Come, O Come, Emmanuel

Plainsong, 13th Century
Words translated by John M. Neale and Henry S. Coffin

O Little Town of Bethlehem

Words by Phillips Brooks
Music by Lewis H. Redner

O Holy Night

French Words by Placide Cappeau
English Words by John S. Dwight
Music by Adolphe Adam

Once in Royal David's City

Words by Cecil F. Alexander
Music by Henry J. Gauntlett

Additional Lyrics

2. He came down to earth from heaven,
   Who is God and Lord of all,
   And His shelter was a stable,
   And His cradle was a stall.
   With the poor, the mean and lowly,
   Lived on earth our Savior holy.

3. Jesus is our childhood's pattern;
   Day by day like us He grew.
   He was little, weak and helpless;
   Tears and smiles, like us, He knew.
   And He feeleth for our sadness,
   And He shareth in our gladness.

4. And our eyes at last shall see Him,
   Through His own redeeming love,
   For that child so dear and gentle
   Is our Lord in heav'n above.
   And He leads His children on
   To the place where He is gone.

Pat-a-Pan
(Willie, Take Your Little Drum)

Words and Music by Bernard de la Monnoye

Silent Night

Words by Joseph Mohr
Translated by John F. Young
Music by Franz X. Gruber

Still, Still, Still

Salzburg Melody, c.1819
Traditional Austrian Text

Star of the East

Words by George Cooper
Music by Amanda Kennedy

1. Star of the east, O Beth - le - hem's star,
2. Star of the east, un - dimmed by each cloud,

guid - ing us on to heav - en a - far.
what though the on storms of grief gath - er loud.

Sor - row and grief are lulled by thy light, thou
Faith - ful and pure, are thy rays' beam to save, still

hope of each mor - tal in death's lone - ly night.
bright o'er each the cra - dle and bright o'er the

Fear - less and tran - quil we look up to thee,

know - ing   thou   beam'st through e - ter - ni - ty.

Help   us   to   fol - low   where   thou   still   dost   guide

D.C. al Coda

pil - grims   of   earth   so   wide. _____

Coda

Outro

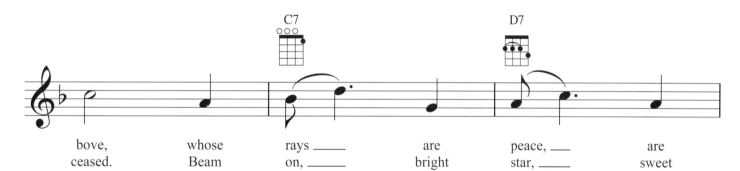

grave.   O   star   that   leads   to   God __ a -
o'er   us   still   till   life __ hath

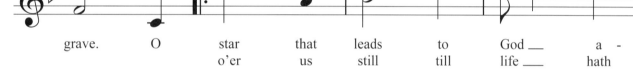

bove,   whose   rays ____   are   peace, ____   are
ceased.   Beam   on, ____   bright   star, ____   sweet

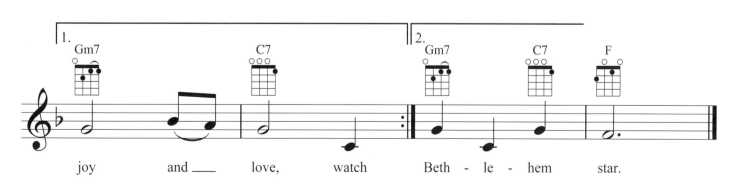

1.
joy   and __ love,   watch

2.
Beth - le - hem   star.

Sussex Carol

Traditional English Carol

First note

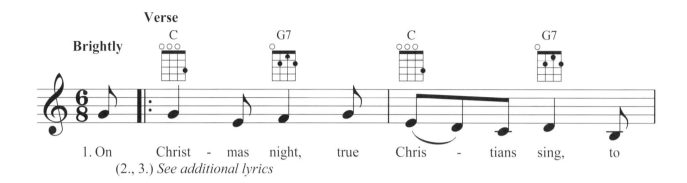

1. On Christ - mas night, true Chris - tians sing, to
(2., 3.) *See additional lyrics*

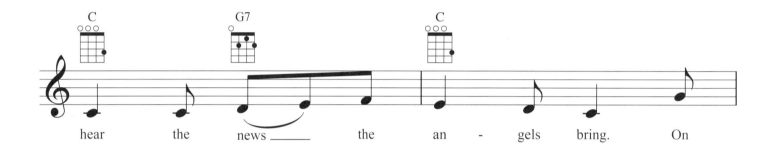

hear the news _____ the an - gels bring. On

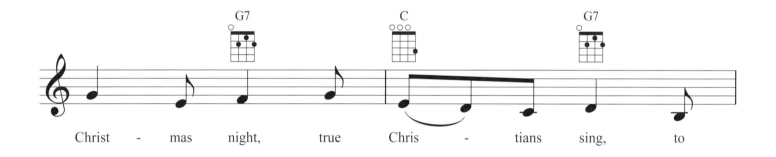

Christ - mas night, true Chris - tians sing, to

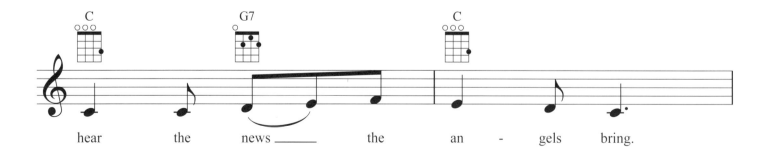

hear the news _____ the an - gels bring.

News   of   great   joy _____ and   of _____ great

mirth,   tid - ings   of   our   dear

Sav - ior's   birth. _____ | 1.–3. | 4.

2. The   ____
3. So
4. From

Additional Lyrics

2. The King of kings to us is giv'n,
    The Lord of earth and King of heav'n.
    The King of kings to us is giv'n,
    The Lord of earth and King of heav'n.
    Angels and men with joy may sing
    Of blest Jesus, their Savior King.

3. So how on earth can men be sad,
    When Jesus comes to make us glad?
    So how on earth can men be sad,
    When Jesus comes to make us glad?
    From all our sins to set us free,
    Buying for us our liberty.

4. From out the darkness have we light,
    Which makes the angels sing this night.
    From out the darkness have we light,
    Which makes the angels sing this night.
    "Glory to God, His peace to men,
    And goodwill evermore, amen."

The Twelve Days of Christmas

Traditional English Carol

Additional Lyrics

8. On the eighth day... eight maids a-milking...
9. On the ninth day... nine ladies dancing...
10. On the tenth day... ten lords a-leaping...
11. On the 'leventh day... 'leven pipers piping...
12. On the twelfth day... twelve drummers drumming...

Ukrainian Bell Carol

Traditional
Arranged by Mykola Leontovych

First note

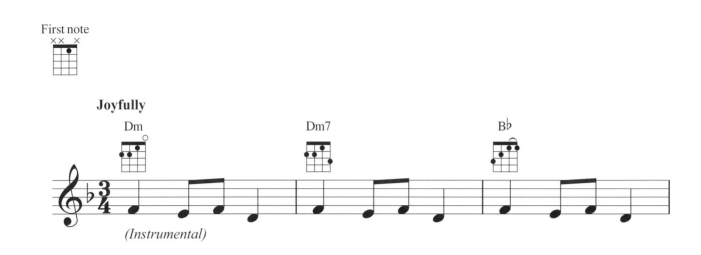

Joyfully

(Instrumental)

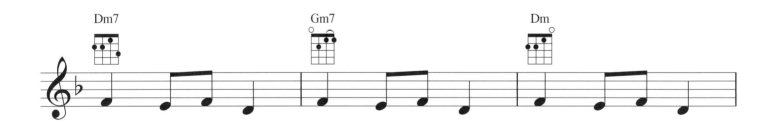

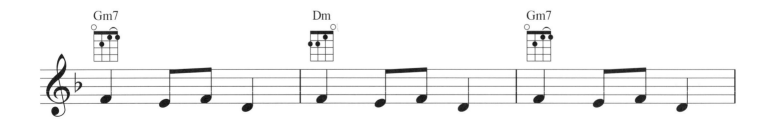

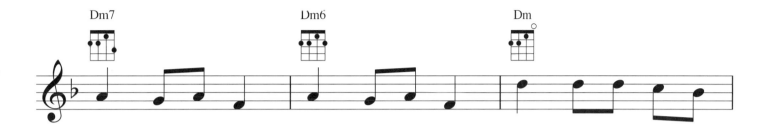

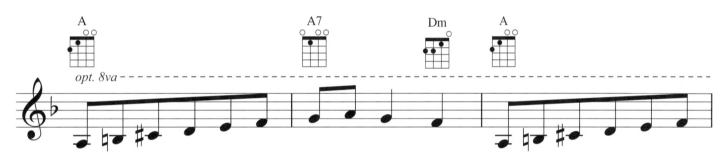

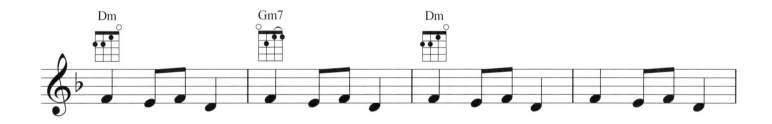

Up on the Housetop

Words and Music by B.R. Hanby

First note

Verse
Playfully, in 2

1. Up on the house - top rein - deer pause. Out jumps good old
2. First comes the stock - ing of lit - tle Nell. Oh, dear San - ta,
3. Next comes the stock - ing of lit - tle Will. Oh, just see what a

San - ta Claus. Down through the chim - ney with lots of toys.
fill it well. Give her a dol - ly that laughs and cries,
glo - rious fill! Here is a ham - mer and lots of tacks,

Chorus

All for the lit - tle ones, Christ - mas joys.
one that will o - pen and shut her eyes.   Ho, ho, ho, who would - n't go?
al - so a ball and a whip that cracks.

Ho, ho, ho, who would - n't go? _____ Up on the house - top,

click, click, click. Down through the chim - ney with good Saint Nick.

We Wish You a Merry Christmas

Traditional English Folksong

First note

Brightly

§ Chorus

F | Bb

We wish you a mer-ry Christ-mas, we

G7 | C | A7

wish you a mer-ry Christ-mas, we wish you a mer-ry

Dm | Bb | C7 | F

To Coda ⊕

Christ-mas and a hap-py New Year. Good

Bridge

Dm | Am | G7 | C | F

tid-ings to you, wher-ev-er you are. Good tid-ings for

D.S. al Coda

C | Bb | C7 | F

⊕ **Coda**

F

Christ-mas and a hap-py New Year. We

Year.

We Three Kings of Orient Are

Words and Music by John H. Hopkins, Jr.

Chorus

O _____ star of won - der, star of night,

star with roy - al beau - ty bright,

west - ward lead - ing, still pro - ceed - ing,

guide us to thy per - fect light. light.

Additional Lyrics

4. Myrrh is mine; its bitter perfume
   Breathes a life of gathering gloom;
   Sorr'wing, sighing, bleeding, dying,
   Sealed in the stone-cold tomb.

5. Glorious now, behold Him arise,
   King and God and sacrifice.
   Alleluia, alleluia,
   Sounds through the earth and skies.

What Child Is This?

Words by William C. Dix
16th Century English Melody

1. What Child is this, _____ who, laid to
(2., 3.) *See additional lyrics*

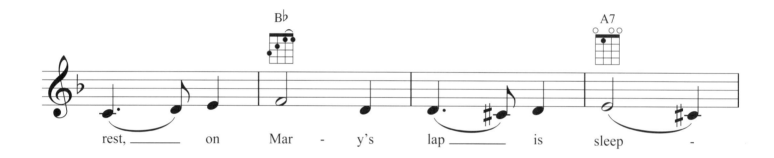

rest, _____ on Mar - y's lap _____ is sleep -

ing; whom an - gels greet ____ with an - thems sweet ____ while

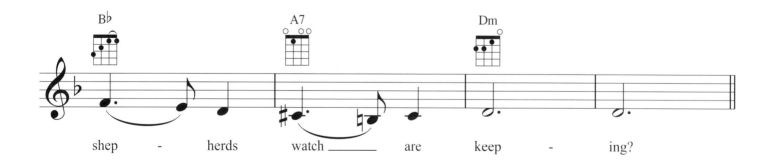

shep - herds watch _____ are keep - ing?

Chorus

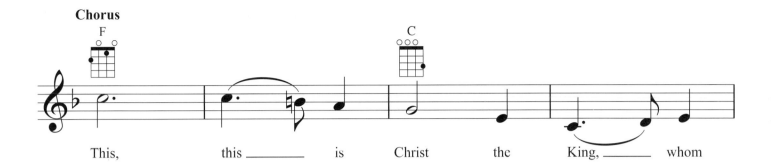

This, this _____ is Christ the King, _____ whom

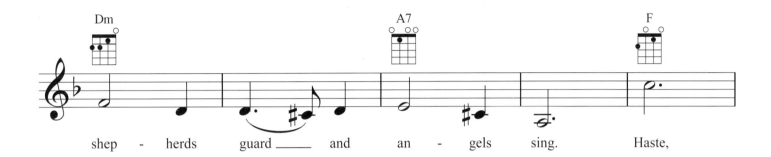

shep - herds guard _____ and an - gels sing. Haste,

haste _____ to bring Him laud, _____ the Babe, _____ the

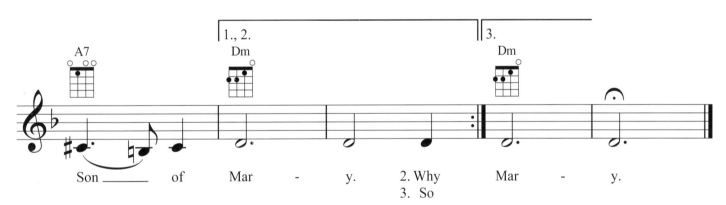

Son _____ of Mar - y. 2. Why Mar - y.
3. So

Additional Lyrics

2. Why lies He in such mean estate
   Where ox and ass are feeding?
   Good Christian, fear, for sinners here
   The silent Word is pleading.

3. So bring Him incense, gold and myrrh.
   Come, peasant, king, to own Him.
   The King of kings salvation brings;
   Let loving hearts enthrone Him.

While Shepherds Watched Their Flocks

Words by Nahum Tate
Music by George Frideric Handel

Additional Lyrics

2. "Fear not!" said he, for mighty dread
   Had seized their troubled mind.
   "Glad tidings of great joy I bring
   To you and all mankind,
   To you and all mankind.

3. "To you, in David's town this day,
   Is born of David's line,
   The Savior, who is Christ the Lord;
   And this shall be the sign,
   And this shall be the sign:

4. "The heavenly Babe you there shall find
   To human view displayed,
   All meanly wrapped in swathing bands,
   And in a manger laid,
   And in a manger laid."

5. Thus spake the seraph; and forthwith
   Appeared a shining throng
   Of angels praising God on high,
   Who thus addressed their song,
   Who thus addressed their song:

6. "All glory be to God on high,
   And to the earth be peace;
   Good will henceforth from heav'n to men,
   Begin and never cease,
   Begin and never cease!"